30
...To Understand the Financial Pages

DONALD WATERS

KOGAN PAGE

First published in the UK by Kogan Page, 2000

Kogan Page Limited
120 Pentonville Road
London N1 9JN

British Library Cataloguing in Publication Data
A CIP record for this book is available from the British Library.

ISBN 0 7494 3282 9

Typeset by Florence Production Ltd, Stoodleigh, Devon

Printed and bound in Great Britain by Clays Ltd, St Ives plc

CONTENTS

PREFACE

Newspapers are full of financial reports. Sometimes the reports are important enough to hit the headlines, but more often they are buried somewhere near the back pages. Many of these reports seem rather obscure (how exactly does yesterday's fall in the Hang Seng index affect us?). Most of them use terms that we do not understand.

But the truth is that we are all affected by the financial markets. When interest rates rise, we pay more for our mortgage; a deal between breweries closes our local pub; a weak dollar reduces our company's exports and we worry about job security; competition between electricity suppliers means that our bills fall.

The problem is that we get lost in the technicalities of finance. What's the difference between debentures and gilts? Are stocks and shares the same? Who uses merchant banks? What exactly is a leveraged buy-out?

This book answers some of these questions. It talks about finance in a clear and straightforward way, without assuming any previous knowledge or expertise.

1

MONEY AND MARKETS

Intermediaries

Suppose that you have been living rather frugally and have managed to save some cash. A lot of other people are short of money, and would like to borrow it. In return, they will pay you interest. To put it formally, you have accumulated **capital**, which you **invest** to earn a **return**. This is the basis of all finance.

Financial markets provide the intermediaries who organize the flow of money between those who want to lend and those who want to borrow. In practice, the major borrowers are governments and companies with long-term expenditure plans, while the lenders are individuals who invest their savings.

Organizing the flow of funds from lenders to borrowers may seem fairly straightforward, but in practice it is immensely complicated. Expert intermediaries have to look after the details – in the same way that estate agents, solicitors and building societies help when you buy a house.

Various types of **finance company** offer a range of services to make the flow of funds as smooth as possible. In the past, each company tended to specialize in a particular type of deal, but recent reorganizations have led to the formation of large **financial conglomerates** offering a full range of financial services.

These finance companies work in an exotic place called **the City**. This is 'the square mile' of the City of London, which is the centre of the UK finance industry. All the major institutions such as the Bank of England, the Stock Exchange and Lloyd's are in this small area. Many finance companies are physically outside the City, so the term simply refers to every organization working in the financial sector. Wall Street is the equivalent area in the USA.

Banks and building societies

When you want to talk about finance, your first call is probably to your bank. You can still find branches on your high street, but electronic banking and mergers are making these rarer. Banks, like Barclays, HSBC and Lloyds-TSB, are the retail or **clearing banks** approved by the **Financial Services Authority (FSA)**. Their main business is looking after customer accounts, clearing payments and organizing short-term deposits and loans. **Merchant banks** offer similar services to companies and the occasional rich individual. You will probably not have much contact with merchant banks, but can see them working to help with large mergers, or raise capital for a takeover.

Building societies specialize in arranging mortgages. They are mutual societies owned by their members – or customers – who share any profits and benefits. In recent years many of the larger societies have demutualized to become banks, and their profits are now distributed to shareholders rather than to customers.

Your bank is happy to help with your finances, but it is usually only an intermediary – acting like an estate agent when you buy a house. If you want to buy shares, for example, the bank passes your request to a stockbroker who makes the actual purchase; if you want life assurance the bank passes your details to an insurance company.

Our access to financial markets is very restricted and we invariably work through intermediaries. If you want to buy shares in Railtrack you do not write to them enclosing a cheque, but contact a financial advisor who works through a stockbroker. In many ways this is a safeguard. Our affairs are looked after by experts – and the markets are safe from meddling amateurs who do not know what they are doing. Of course, it also means that we pay fees for services we do not really want. Buying shares is fairly straightforward, but we have to work through intermediaries and pay each one a commission.

Interest and present values

Investing means that you give up money now in return for payments at some point in the future. These future payments must be big enough to make your investment worth while. But how do you know its future value? You can work this out by looking at the interest it earns.

Interest is the reward you get for lending money. If you invest £100 at an annual interest rate of 10 per cent, at the end of the year you have $100 \times 1.1 = £110$. If you keep the money invested, at the end of the second year you have $110 \times 1.1 = £121$. This is the principle of **compound interest** where you get interest on both your original investment and on the interest that has already accumulated.

Interest of 10 per cent means that £100 now will be worth £110 in a year's time. Another way of looking at this is to say that £110 in a year's time has the same value as £100 now. You can use this idea to **discount** future amounts of money to give their present value.

Interest rates

Interest rates are usually quoted as an annual percentage, so it should be easy to compare them. Unfortunately, you can calculate the amount you actually get (or pay) in slightly different ways. This is why all borrowers and lenders have to quote a standard **Annual Percentage Rate (APR)**, which shows the amount a borrower actually pays each year for a loan. An APR of 7.8% means that a person borrowing £100 for a year repays a total of £107.80.

There are also other complications, such as income tax. Investors are often paid interest net of income tax, so the standard rate of tax is withheld and paid directly to the government. In this case companies can describe interest rates as '6 per cent net, equivalent to 7.2 per cent gross'.

There are so many different kinds of investments that, even with APRs, it is difficult to compare them. The only consistent feature is that when you borrow money the interest rate is much higher than when you invest it. A high street bank may pay you 5 per cent to deposit money, but will charge you 13 per cent to borrow it. The difference covers overheads, risks, fees and related costs. As banks generally make huge profits, you may wonder why the difference between lending and borrowing rates is so high. The simple answer is that they can get away with it. This, in turn, makes people ask if there really is fierce competition in the banking sector.

In practice, there can be more flexibility with loans than with deposits, and it is always worth negotiating the conditions. Remember that lenders are not doing you a favour – this is what they are in business to do.

The amount of interest you get from an investment depends on:

- general market conditions and prevailing interest rates;
- the amount of risk you are prepared to take;
- how long you want to invest for, with longer terms getting higher interest rates; and
- how much you want to invest, with bigger sums getting more interest.

Your attitude towards risk is particularly important here. Interest is often seen as a reward for taking risks, so higher rewards come from higher risks. Putting money in a bank account is very safe, and you get relatively low returns; on the other hand, putting money into a new business is very risky, and you would expect higher returns (or, of course, you may lose everything).

Prevailing interest rates

The main factor that sets your expected return from investments is the prevailing interest rate. Some people imagine that this is set by the supply and demand for money. When more people want to borrow than to invest, demand for money exceeds supply and interest rates rise; when more people want to invest than to borrow, the supply of money exceeds demand and interest rates fall.

In reality, the interest rates are set by government policy. To put it simply, the government believes that low interest rates lead to inflation. They encourage people to borrow more – thus increasing the demand for goods and the amount of money in circulation. This rise in economic activity might seem good, but prices inevitably rise and lead to higher inflation. On the other hand, high interest rates discourage borrowing, and reduce the demand for goods and the supply of money. This controls inflation, but also limits economic growth.

The government sets targets that balance inflation and economic growth. It passes these to the **Bank of England** – sometimes called the 'Old Lady of Threadneedle Street', or simply 'the Bank' – which actually sets the interest rates.

Since 1997, the Bank's **Monetary Policy Committee (MPC)** has met once a month to set the official rate at which the Bank provides funds to the banking system. Their decisions are not based on precise calculation, but use a bit of analysis, a bit of theory, a bit of judgement and a lot of guesswork. They have to balance economic growth and inflation, as well as international interest rates, currency exchange rates, growth in wages, balance of payments, investment rates, optimism in the economy, and so on. Nominally, the MPC acts independently, but it has to meet the government's economic targets and so has little room to manoeuvre.

The Bank's official rate sets the context for all other interest rates. When it is announced, other finance companies set their **base rate** (called the prime rate in the USA), which is the rate they use to calculate borrowing and lending rates. Government and local authorities might borrow money at 0.5 per cent above base rate; large, safe companies – known as blue chip companies – might borrow money at 1 per cent above base rate; individuals and smaller companies might pay 6 per cent above base rate. If you put money into an instant access bank account you might receive 1.5 per cent under base rate.

Banks and other finance companies act independently, so it is a remarkable coincidence that they always work with the same base rates. Occasionally a smaller bank may use a slightly higher base rate to attract business, but there is no significant variation.

The Bank of England

The Bank acts as an intermediary between the government and the City. As a central bank – like the Federal Reserve in the USA, the Bundesbank in Germany and the Bank of Japan – its main functions are to:

- act as banker to the government – holding the government's deposits of revenues and reserves, and using these to pay bills. It also issues bonds to cover government debts;

- act as banker to the banks – taking deposits from commercial banks and controlling the supply of money to keep the financial system stable. Here it is the lender of last resort, giving loans to banks that have short-term difficulties with cash supply;

- regulate commercial banks – although this function has largely been passed to the Financial Services Authority;

- stabilize exchange rates – through intervention in the currency markets;

- issue currency; and

- set the official interest rate.

Other interest rates

Very large loans are linked to the **London Inter-Bank Offered Rate (LIBOR)** rather than the base rate. LIBOR is the rate at which banks lend money to each other. It is the rate a bank would itself have to pay to acquire a large amount of cash, so you can imagine it as the whole-sale price of cash. The base rate is changed relatively infrequently and is strongly influenced by government policies, but LIBOR moves continuously to reflect market conditions.

Table 1.1 Examples of London Money Rates

1	2	3	4	5	6	7
	Over-night	*7 Days' Notice*	*One Month*	*Three Months*	*Six Months*	*One Year*
Inter-bank Sterling	5⅛–3⅞	4⅞–4½	5⅞–5½	6⅛ –5⅜	6⅜–6¼	6⅞–6¾
Local Authority Deposits	5¼–5	5⅜–5	5¾–5⅜	6⅜–6	6½–6⅜	7–6⅞
Treasury Bills	–	–	5⅞–5¾	5⅞–5¾	–	–

Table 1.1 shows an extract from a published table of London Money Rates. These tables show the current interest rates for different types of loan.

Column 1 shows the type of loan. Inter-bank sterling, local authority deposits, treasury bills and other types are effectively IOUs issued by different types of organization. Columns 2 to 7 show the rates that apply to loans of different duration, with longer-term loans generally having higher rates than shorter-term ones.

There are two figures for each entry: a higher one showing the rate a bank will lend at and a lower one showing the rate it will borrow at. The difference between these two – the **spread** – allows the bank to make a profit and also suggests the level of risk involved in the loan. The greater the perceived risk, the wider the spread, with the very safe wholesale market having small margins.

Interest rates are sometimes given in unusual ways, such as 5¹⁄₃₂ per cent. The reasons for this are largely historical, but they show the importance of small changes. Finance companies invest huge amounts of money, and a tiny difference in rates can make a big difference to profits. They often quote price differences in **basis points**, which are hundredths of a per cent. The difference between 5.53 per cent and 5.87 per cent is 34 basis points.

You can compare these interest rates with domestic rates in other countries. The most common figures quoted are the official rates, usually abbreviated to a middle rate, which comes halfway between the buying and selling rates. Table 1.2 shows an extract from one table. As well as the current short-term rate, this shows the rate for three-month loans and gives an idea of how this rate has changed in the past year.

Any international comparisons are very difficult. Economic situations in different countries vary so much that you have to understand the context of the figures, and remember that higher interest rates normally come with higher risks. If a bank is paying depositors 55 per cent a year, there must be a reason for this apparent generosity.

Table 1.2 International interest rates

	Official Short Term	Three-month Rate			
		Current Level	Change in Week	Year High	Year Low
UK	5.75	6.16	0.00	7.64	4.97
USA	5.75	6.04	+0.04	6.28	4.86
Japan	0.50	0.15	+0.05	0.88	0.05
Euro	3.25	3.49	0.00	3.53	2.50

2

COMPANIES, SHARES AND PROFITS

Organizing a business

If you work for yourself, you can run your business as a **sole trader**. Alternatively, you can work with other people in a **partnership**. With both of these you – and any partners – supply the capital for the business, and are responsible for all its operations. In particular, you are personally responsible for all the business's liabilities, and if you hit problems you have to pay all the debts yourself.

An alternative is to form a **limited liability company**. This is a separate legal entity, which exists by itself and is distinct from its owners. The behaviour of a company is controlled by a stream of laws that cover everything from the name it can use to the way it treats its employees. A company's **Articles of Association** are like a constitution – they form a contract between the company and its shareholders. The Registrar of Companies records all this information in Companies House.

The Articles of Association include routine information about the company, including the number of **shares** it can issue. Investors buy these shares and their payments form the company's working capital. A family company might have four shareholders; BT has millions.

The advantage of this arrangement is that each shareholder has limited liability. The company has a separate existence, and if it runs into problems the liability of each shareholder is limited to the amount they paid for their shares. If the company loses money, shareholders can lose the money they spent on shares, but they do not have to pay any more to cover the company's debts.

There are two types of company: **private companies** and **public limited companies (plcs)**. Private companies usually have 'limited' after their name. Shares are not traded on any market, and you cannot buy them unless invited. These are typically family businesses where all the shares are owned by family members, or subsidiaries where the shares are owned by another company. Public limited company shares are openly traded on a market, such as the London Stock Exchange, and anyone can buy them.

Owners

The shareholders own a company. Most shares are **ordinary shares** (called common stock in the USA), which have equal status. Sometimes, there are preference shares, which have some priority over the ordinary shares, perhaps giving a minimum dividend.

In return for putting money into the company by buying shares – the **equity capital** – the shareholders receive profits distributed through **dividends** and they have some say in how the business is run. Each ordinary share has one vote in company business. However, Tesco has seven billion shares; if you own a few shares in a major company you own a tiny part of it and have very little say in its operations.

15

When one company wants to take over another, it offers to buy shares at a premium above their current price. Their aim is to acquire more than 51 per cent of shares, giving them effective control of the company. There are many rules for takeovers of plcs, such as a company acquiring more than 30 per cent of the shares in another company has to put in a bid for all the remaining shares. You will often hear that one company has acquired 29.9 per cent of another, thus avoiding the problem of having to bid for the whole company.

Not surprisingly, large companies usually take over smaller ones. Sometimes there is a **reverse takeover**, when a small company can raise the cash to buy a larger one. This is usually a **leveraged buy-out**, where the small company borrows most of the money it needs. Not all shareholders sell, and they keep a minority interest in the company.

Managers

Shareholders do not look after the day-to-day operations of a company, instead they hire **directors** to do this for them. The shareholders can exert their influence by voting to appoint or dismiss certain directors, or voting on some major operational change, but they rarely get involved in company decisions. If shareholders do not like the way a company is run, they are much more likely to sell their shares than try to change things.

The senior managers responsible for running a company form the **board of directors**. The person in overall charge is the **chief executive**, with the managing director and chairman of the board closely involved – or even the same person. The directors who work for the company form its **executive directors**. Experienced people working for other companies are invited to help the board make decisions, and these are the **non-executive directors**.

Company accounts

Every year company directors produce a set of accounts, which they present to shareholders at the **Annual General Meeting (AGM)**. They describe performance over the past year, and say what plans they have for the future. Usually the shareholders are reasonably happy and these meetings pass with little debate. Occasionally there are problems and the meetings become more heated.

The main contents of the accounts are:

- **profit and loss account** – showing the overall profit (or loss) from normal operations during the year;

- **balance sheet** – giving a snapshot of the company's assets and liabilities at the end of the year; and

- **cash-flow statement** – recording the actual, rather than notional, receipts and payments during the year.

The company directors are responsible for the annual accounts, so the shareholders appoint **auditors** to check them. Auditors are independent accountants who make sure that the published accounts give a true and fair view of the company's performance, and stick to established conventions. In practice, auditors work closely with directors, cannot investigate the figures, and have little chance of discovering any problems.

Profits (and losses)

Shareholders are primarily concerned with the **profit** made by their company. All companies sell products – the combination of goods and services that satisfies customer demand. If customers like a company's products, they buy them at a price that is higher than the production costs. When you subtract all the costs of running the business from the income generated from sales, you are left with the profit. The company retains some of this profit to plough back into future activities, and the rest is distributed to shareholders through a dividend paid on each share.

If the total income does not cover its costs, the company makes a loss. It can survive for some time by borrowing money, but eventually the cash runs out and it starts to default on debts. If the longer-term future of the company does not look too bad, the creditors may agree to **appoint an administrator** to temporarily take over the company and arrange for the debts to be paid. However, if the company's situation looks gloomier, one of the creditors will appoint a **receiver** to recover a debt. Receivers might try to pull a company through its problems, but they usually just sell the assets to recover as much money as possible. After this, the company ceases trading and is wound up – individuals go bankrupt, but companies **go into liquidation**.

It might seem fairly easy to measure a company's profit, but if you look at any set of company accounts you begin to see the complications. You might consider:

- **Profit before interest and tax** = sales − operating costs. The operating costs are directly incurred in making products and running the business.
- **Profit before tax** = profit before interest and tax − interest paid to lenders.
- **Profit after tax** = profit before tax − tax paid to the government.
- **Retained earnings** = profit after tax − dividends paid to shareholders.

The profit after tax is sometimes called the company's **earnings** and, like the other figures, it does not really say much about the company. If Bill's Car Repairs makes a million pounds profit after tax, it would be a miracle – but if Vodafone makes a million pound profit, it would be a disaster. It makes more sense to relate the profit to the size of the company. There are several ways of doing this.

- **Profit margin**: this gives the profit before tax as a percentage of sales:

$$\text{profit margin} = \frac{\text{profit before tax}}{\text{sales}} \times 100$$

- **Return on total assets**: the assets of a company are all the items of value that it owns. These are either: fixed assets (such as land, buildings, equipment, long-term investments and goodwill); or current assets (such as stocks, cash and amounts owed by traders).

$$\text{return on total assets} = \frac{\text{profit before interest and tax}}{\text{fixed assets + current assets}} \times 100$$

This is arguably the most comprehensive measure of business performance, but you have to remember that different types of company need very different amounts of assets. An advertising agency needs few assets and should have a much higher return on assts than a car manufacturer. A good return on total assets is generally in the range of 12 to 18 per cent.

- **Return on equity**: a company gets money from three sources:
  - selling shares to get equity capital;
  - borrowing through loans; and
  - retaining profit to plough back into the business.

The return on equity shows, as a percentage, the profit that could be returned to shareholders:

$$\text{return on equity} = \frac{\text{profit after tax}}{\text{shareholders' money}} \times 100$$

Return on equity is usually a bit higher than return on total assets, and a good value is in the range of 14 to 20 per cent.

Other measures

There are literally hundreds of ways you can measure the performance of a company. Each of these is useful in certain circumstances, but none of them tells the whole story. Two measures that are particularly important for shareholders are **earnings per share** (which shows how much profit shareholders *could* get for each share) and **dividends per share** (which shows how much they *actually* get):

$$\text{earnings per share} = \frac{\text{profit after tax}}{\text{number of shares}}$$

$$\text{dividends per share} = \frac{\text{amount distributed as dividends}}{\text{number of shares}}$$

A related figure shows the **dividend cover**, which is the number of times a company's after-tax profits is greater than the dividends it pays to shareholders. High values – about two – show that the dividend is safe:

$$\text{dividend cover} = \frac{\text{profit after tax}}{\text{profit distributed to shareholders}}$$

A useful picture often comes from the ratio of liquid assets to liabilities, shown in the **acid test**:

$$\text{acid test} = \frac{\text{liquid assets (cash and readily saleable assets)}}{\text{current liabilities}}$$

People take different views of these tests. One view is that an acid test of less than about ½ means that the company may have difficulty dealing with sudden problems. Another very rough guideline says that a company's current liabilities minus its short-term assets should give a value about equal to one year's pre-tax profit.

One measure that is directly related to a company's capital structure is its gearing. This ratio (called 'leverage' in the USA) shows the amount of borrowed money as a percentage of shareholders' money:

$$\text{gearing} = \frac{\text{borrowed money}}{\text{shareholders' money}} \times 100$$

When a company borrows money, it has to pay interest and repay the debt at some agreed point – but it does not have to repay the money it gets from shareholders' equity, or even pay interest. There is a lot of debate about the best balance of debt and equity. In general, when a highly geared company is doing well, it is better to be a shareholder, since the profits are divided between fewer shares; when the company is doing badly it is better to be owed money as the debts have to be paid first, even when there is not enough profit left for dividends.

3

STOCK MARKETS AND EXCHANGES

Stock exchanges

A company's Articles of Association provide some routine information, including the number of shares it can issue and the nominal value of each one. Companies do not usually issue all of their authorized shares, but keep some in reserve. The nominal value is typically 20p or £1, but this has little practical meaning.

Public limited companies – the plcs – raise capital by selling shares to the public. This is organized through a **stock exchange** or **stock market**, which allows companies wanting to sell shares to meet investors wanting to buy them. Most countries, from Argentina to Zimbabwe, have a stock market, and the UK has the **London Stock Exchange** (LSE) with its headquarters in Throgmorton Street. This is the third largest in the world after New York and Tokyo. The stock exchange in Paris is 'the Bourse', and this is often used as a general term for all stock exchanges.

Stock exchanges deal in several types of securities, but for the moment we will stick to ordinary shares. People often use the terms 'stocks' and 'shares' to mean the same thing. There are some technical differences (you can, for example, buy fractions of stocks) but in practice they are virtually the same.

The LSE does not deal with shares of every plc. About 2,200 UK companies and 500 foreign companies are **listed** on the LSE. To be listed, a company has to meet certain conditions. These include publication of full annual accounts, with half-yearly reports on profits. Listed companies produce interim profit statements – including the interim dividend – at the half year; then at the end of the full year they publish a preliminary announcement of performance, with the full, audited accounts coming shortly afterwards.

Launching shares

A new plc has to offer its shares to the public. It is not easy to become a plc, and is even more difficult to be listed on the stock exchange, so it is misleading to call these 'new companies'. They are more likely to be established companies looking to expand. They **offer** their shares to the public – or **launch** them – in one of four ways:

1. **Offer for sale**, with a prospectus describing shares that are offered directly to the public through advertisements;

2. **Offer through intermediaries**, with shares offered to various financial intermediaries who offer them on to their clients;

3. **Placing**, where shares are offered privately to selected investors, perhaps existing clients of the company; or

4. **Introduction**, where a private company already has a spread of shareholders, and is going public without issuing any more shares.

Only the first of these offers shares directly to the public, while the others offer shares through yet more intermediaries. The shares on offer are usually a mixture of shares sold by existing shareholders and new shares issued by the company.

Setting a price for new shares is difficult. In principle, the value of each share is the total value of the company divided by the number of shares. Unfortunately, it is virtually impossible to agree a value on a working company. You can see this clearly when one company makes a hostile bid for another, and there is wide disagreement about the value of the victim.

Merchant banks usually organize the launch of shares, and they tend to suggest prices that are on the low side. This encourages interest in the shares and makes sure that they are all sold. Sometimes the resulting demand is too high and the issue is **over-subscribed**. Investors then get an allocation of shares that usually favours smaller shareholders. Sometimes a share issue is **under-subscribed**, which means that shares are not sold. To safeguard themselves against this risk, companies ask the merchant bank sponsoring the launch to underwrite the shares. This means that – in return for a fee – the merchant bank buys any remaining shares, and either keeps them to sell when the price rises, or sells them at an immediate loss.

Secondary markets

When you buy shares in a company, you do not want your money tied-up forever. You need some means of selling the shares and moving on to new ventures. Sometimes, companies themselves are happy to buy back shares, but usually you look for other people to buy them. This is the important feature of plcs; whenever you want to, you can sell the shares to someone else. The situation with private companies is different, and there may be more conditions on sales.

As you can see, the stock exchange is really two markets: a **primary market** where companies sell new shares to investors and a **secondary market** where investors buy and sell the shares among themselves.

Most of the business in a stock exchange is investors buying and selling shares among themselves. These deals used to be made by the **open outcry** system, with people meeting on the floor of the exchange, shouting and gesticulating in apparent chaos. Electronic trading has changed this and most deals are now made by quietly typing messages to a computer system.

Millions of people own shares in companies, but individual holdings are usually quite small. More often we invest through life assurance policies, occupational pension schemes and managed unit trusts (called 'mutual funds' in the USA). Together, these three own more than 60 per cent of shares listed on the London Stock Exchange.

If you take a typical blue chip company such as Tesco plc, there are almost 200,000 shareholders, who own 7 billion shares. Of these, over 100,000 shareholders own less than 1,000 shares each (meaning that 51 per cent of the shareholders together own 0.33 per cent of the shares). At the other end of the scale, 600 shareholders own more than a million shares each (meaning that the largest 0.3 per cent of shareholders own 83 per cent of the shares).

Share value

Suppose you buy a £1 share in a new company. Over time the company grows. It pays you an annual dividend, and it also ploughs back profits to increase its value. As the company's assets grow, your share becomes worth more than the £1 you originally paid. In other words, you have the benefit of both dividends and **capital growth**. The company might only pay dividends of 5 per cent a year, but if this is combined with a capital increase of 10 per cent then the overall return is a healthy 15 per cent.

Of course, your company will not necessarily expand, and it could join the long list of those that experience financial problems. Then you have the double blow of smaller dividends and a lower market value for your shares. The lower share price may not be a problem until you want to sell your shares, but it certainly is not good news. If the company does not recover, it may eventually cease trading and go into liquidation, when its assets will be sold and distributed to its debtors. Shareholders are at the back of the queue for any remaining cash, but by the time all other debts are repaid there is seldom much cash remaining. The good news is that limited liability means that you do not have to find more cash to cover any remaining debts.

One interesting aspect of trading on the stock exchange is the **settlement time**. People buying shares have to pay for them within five days. This adds some flexibility to deals, as speculators can sell shares that they do not yet own, provided that they can get hold of them before they are due to complete the deal. If they think that a share price will rise, they can agree to buy shares at the current price – but without handing over any cash. If the share price then rises over the next day or so, they can sell the shares at a higher price and simply pocket their profit. Alternatively, if they think a share price will fall, they can sell shares that they do not actually own, and buy them in the next few days at a lower price. This **selling short** involves the obvious risk that the share prices do not act as expected.

Dealers in the market

Deregulation in recent years has removed many of the traditional barriers between jobs in the stock market. But this does not mean that anyone can link into the stock exchange's computer and start dealing. The stock exchange is run by specialists, and we always have to deal through intermediaries.

At the heart of the stock exchange is the group of 30 or so **market-makers**. These are the people (who used to be called 'jobbers') who risk their own money in the buying and selling of shares. They are now branches of financial conglomerates which make a profit by trading in shares.

On the stock market's computers, market-makers display the prices at which they are willing to buy, the prices at which they are willing to sell, and the size of deal they will consider. This effectively sets the price of every share and gives a view of current market conditions. The market-makers get a profit from their spread – offering to buy at a lower price than they are willing to sell. They anticipate demand for shares, and adjust their prices and spread accordingly to give a **turn** or profit.

The main system for these deals is the **Stock Exchange Automated Quotations System (SEAQ)**. Every market-maker, stockbroker and larger financial institutions have access to the SEAQ. This automatically handles small deals, and monitors the market by recording the size, time and price of every deal made.

The stock exchange has a 'quote-driven' system, which is based on the quotes given by market-makers. An alternative 'order-driven' system would remove the need for market-makers and have buyers and sellers talking directly to each other, saying what they want to do and at what price. This approach is used in other exchanges, and has been partly introduced with the **Stock Exchange Electronic Trading Service (SETS)**. This gives an automatic system for some transactions, particularly for shares in major companies.

Most of us cannot access the SEAQ or SETS and have no connection to the stock exchange's computers. We have to work through stockbrokers, who organize the buying and selling of shares. In theory, they search through the SEAQ and then use their expertise to make the best possible deal for us – but in practice their job has become little more than pressing the appropriate keys on a computer system. Stockbrokers make their money by charging a commission on each deal.

Other stock markets

Newer or smaller companies, which cannot meet the requirements of full listing on LSE, can be quoted in other markets. For example, the LSE has a second tier of companies on their **Alternative Investment Market (AIM)**, which replaced the short-lived Unlisted Securities Market. Similarly, **OFEX**, or 'Off Exchange', is a facility set up in 1995 by the stockbrokers J P Jenkins, which allows dealing in shares of about 200 unlisted companies. These facilities allow small and young companies to find a market for their shares, but investments here can be risky.

If you are looking for more exotic deals, you do not have to trade in London, but can buy shares anywhere from

Adelaide to Zurich. You can get all the information you need from the World Wide Web and do the trades electronically. Of course, it may take some courage to start, and will need some specialized knowledge. A useful starting point is the National Association of Securities Dealers Automated Quotations – more usually abbreviated to **NASDAQ**. This is the world's fourth largest stock exchange, listing about 5,000 companies with a market value of £3.2 trillion. Set up in 1971, it concentrates on high-technology companies, such as Microsoft and Intel, and aims to become the first global stock exchange. There are several other electronic markets including **EASDAQ** and **EURO.NM**.

4

SHARE PRICES

Supply and demand

Each share of a company has a nominal par value, perhaps
20p or £1. But this has no relation to its actual value, and
in the USA many shares do not even have a par value. We
could get a realistic value for a share by dividing the total
value of the company by the number of shares issued.
Unfortunately, as we have already mentioned, it is difficult
to put a realistic value on a working company. In practice,
we usually work the other way around and find the value
of a company from its share price. Multiplying the number
of shares issued by the price of each gives the company's
value; or its **market capitalization**.

When shares are launched on to the market they have
an offer price, but afterwards their price is set by market-
makers responding to market forces. They display two
prices: the **offer price**, which is the higher price at which
they will sell, and the **bid price**, which is the lower price
at which they will buy. Between these is the **middle price**,
which is the one that is generally published. When you see

a share price, remember that this is not the price at which you can expect to buy or sell, and do not forget other little details such as stockbrokers' commissions, stamp duty and capital gains tax.

But what sets the share price? It is reassuring to find that share prices react to supply and demand. When brokers start buying large numbers of a particular share, market-makers adjust the offer price upwards; on the other hand, they adjust the bid price downwards when they have difficulty selling a share. Of course, this raises the related question of 'Why do people start buying a particular share?' This is more difficult to answer, but the underlying theme is that investors expect the shares to rise in value. They buy shares now so that they can sell them later at a profit. There are several reasons why a share might rise in value:

- **Takeovers**: when one company tries to take over another, it has to pay a premium above the current share price.

- **Rumours of takeovers** are enough make some prices soar.

- **Tips**: advice to buy or sell a share in a newspaper has a dramatic affect on its price.

- **Consistent growth**: a history of continued growth suggests that the share value will continue to rise in the future.

- **High profits**: if a company reported higher profits than expected, its share price might suddenly rise.

- **Changing interest rates**: in general, high interest rates reduce economic activity and depress share prices.

- **Following other markets**: share prices in one market, say London, tend to follow those in another, say New York.

- **Market manoeuvres**: market-makers and stock-brokers need continuing deals to make a profit. When things look a little lethargic, they may adjust prices to stimulate activity.

- **Shortage of shares**: speculators can sell shares that they do not yet own, under the assumption that prices will fall and they can buy the shares before it is time to settle. If they misjudge things, they may have to buy shares quickly whatever the price.

- **Automatic responses**: many companies have systems that track share prices, and when they see certain patterns – such as a price that goes out of a specified range – they send an automatic signal to buy or sell.

- **Cycles**: there are cycles in share prices which are not well understood – just like general business cycles.

- **Random factors**: many price changes simply cannot be explained – perhaps people feel better on a sunny day, share prices gather a momentum, or the 'feel-good factor' is at work.

Quoted prices

Many factors affect share prices, but we have no real idea of the mechanisms involved. A share is only worth what someone else will pay for it. Unfortunately, this is a volatile figure that changes from day to day, and even from minute to minute. Sometimes there is a clear reason for a change, but we are often lost for an explanation. The only thing for certain is that if we could predict the value of even a single share, we could soon become very rich.

Many analysts continuously scan share prices looking for patterns and trends. They can often forecast likely events, particularly if they know a lot about the company and its general industry. If, for example, a company is likely to publish high profits, the market is aware of this some time in advance. Then the share price will rise before the results are actually published. In other words, the price rise that would normally come after the announcement has been **discounted**, and by the time the good results are announced there is no scope for a further rise. Many investors will now start profit-taking and selling their shares, thus reducing the price. This is the reason why the publication of good results is often associated with a fall in share price. When you hear about 'unexpected moves in the City' it means that something came as a surprise and there had been no discounting.

It is sometimes a very small step from analysing the markets (which is clever) to **insider trading** (which is illegal). It is against the law for anyone to deal in shares if they have confidential information that is not available to the people they are dealing with. This means that directors, employees, accountants, consultants and advisors cannot use confidential information they have about their company to buy or sell shares at the best time. Unfortunately, the tiny number of prosecutions shows that this law is virtually impossible to enforce. There seem to be regular cases of abuse where directors (or more likely their family and friends) buy shares immediately before a jump in price.

We cannot suggest a reasonable share price, but there is an obvious minimum. Suppose that the share price falls until it is much lower than the net assets per share. Then anyone buying the company would get a bargain, as they could sell the assets of the company for more than they paid. This is known as **asset stripping**. Asset strippers have got a bad name, as they seem to do little more than close down viable companies, sell the assets and sack the employees.

Table 4.1 Illustration of share price listing

1	2	3	4	5	6	7	8	9	10	11	12	13
Name	Notes	Price			Mark Cap	EPS	P/E	Divi-dend	Divi-dend Cover	Yield	ROE	Price Index
		Current	Hi	Lo								
National Grid plc		452	518	384	6705	24.76	18.2	13.1	1.8	3.3	18.8	0.948

Table 4.2 Illustration of indices for the French stock exchange

Index	Latest Close	Yesterday's Close	Previous Close	Year High	Year Low	Yield	P/E
SBF 250	3573.98	3512.81	3527.24	3810.86	2507.84	1.9	22.8
CAC 40	5539.61	5450.11	5479.70	5958.32	3958.72	–	–

Company performance

Share prices are widely published in newspapers, magazines, television, the Web, and a variety of information services. As well as basic prices, you can find a lot of other information, and Table 4.1 shows part of a typical listing. Here we have taken – entirely at random – National Grid plc. Remember that these reports pack a lot of information into a small space, so you will meet a lot of abbreviations and codes.

In Table 4.1, you can see that:

- Column 1 is the company name.
- Column 2 gives some notes, perhaps showing that the company has just paid a dividend, or has published interim results. If you buy shares 'ex-dividend' it means that you do not get the next dividend, which is kept by the seller.
- Column 3 is the current share price in pence – remember that this is the middle price between bid and offer prices, and is often the price at the close of the previous day's trading.
- Columns 4 and 5 give an indication of price changes. Here the highest and lowest price over the past year are shown, though the price change in the last working day might be shown instead.
- Column 6 is the market capitalization in millions of pounds – which is the share price multiplied by the number of shares issued.
- Column 7 shows the earnings per share, which is the profit after tax divided by the number of shares.
- Column 8 is the price-to-earnings ratio.

$$\text{price-to-earnings ratio} = \frac{\text{share price}}{\text{earnings per share}}$$

This ratio shows what investors think of the share. If the P/E ratio is high, ie around 20, investors think that the share price is likely to rise in the future. A low ratio means that investors are less confident that the company will continue growing.

- Column 9 shows the latest dividend paid per share in pence.

- Column 10 shows the dividend cover, which is the number of times the net profit is greater than the amount paid in dividends.

- Column 11 is the **yield**, which is the current dividend as a percentage of share price:

$$\text{yield} = \frac{\text{dividend}}{\text{share price}} \times 100$$

One school of thought says that fast-growing companies have high share values and lower yields, while those whose growth is less certain have low share prices and high yields. You should treat this advice with caution. The company decides exactly how much of the profits to return in dividends: if it is mean one year and retains more profit, the yield goes down, but this does not necessarily mean that the company will suddenly enjoy faster growth. Notice that the yield and P/E ratio move in opposite directions – if the share price rises, the yield falls and the P/E ratio rises.

- Column 12 shows the return on equity, which is the after-tax profits divided by the shareholders' funds.

- Column 13 shows the current value of £1 invested in the share a year ago.

Scrip issues and rights

For some reason, investors do not seem to like buying high-priced shares – they prefer to buy 100 shares at £2 each than 2 shares at £100 each. If a company finds that its share price is rising too high, it can simply issue more shares to its existing shareholders. A **scrip issue** – also called a bonus or capitalization issue – gives existing shareholders more shares at no extra cost. This is not an act of generosity, as the share price obviously adjusts: a one-for-one scrip issue will double the number of shares everybody has and halve the share price. There are some accounting benefits to these arrangements, but they are largely cosmetic exercises.

A related way of adjusting the share value is through a **rights issue**. With this, the company raises capital by selling new or unissued shares to its existing shareholders. As a reward, they are usually sold at a discount below current market price. The pricing of a rights issue has to be done carefully, as the extra new shares will automatically reduce their current market price.

Bulls, bears and indices

Some factors affecting prices are only relevant to a single share – such as anticipated profits – while other factors affect the whole market – such as prevailing interest rates. Widespread changes allow commentators to say things like 'the market responded favourably to the news', which means that average share prices rose. When there is general optimism and share prices rise it is called a **bull market**: when there is general pessimism and share prices fall it is called a **bear market**. No one is quite sure of the origin of these terms, but it is easy to remember that bears knock people down, while bulls toss them up into the air.

When speculators are bullish about a share they **go long**, buying shares to sell them later at a profit: when they are bearish they **go short**, selling shares they do not yet own, gambling that they can buy them cheaper before it is time to deliver.

Rather than talk vaguely about rising or falling share prices, it is useful to have some measure of the overall market condition. This is given by a financial index, which is simply the current price divided by the price on a specific date (the **base** price). This ratio is usually multiplied by 100 to give a convenient number:

$$\text{index} = \frac{\text{current price}}{\text{base price}} \times 100$$

In London the most common indices are the **Financial Times Actuaries Share Indices**. The Financial Times Ordinary Share Index (the **FT Index**) follows the share price of 30 large companies in a spread of industries. It was started at 100 in 1935 and now has a value of around 4,000 – showing that, on average, these share prices have risen to 40 times their original prices.

A slightly broader picture comes from the **FTSE 100 index** – the 'Footsie' – which follows the share prices of 100 leading companies (generally considered to be the blue chip companies). This was started at 1,000 in 1984, and now has a value of around 6,500. You can find a whole range of such indices, including the FTSE 250 index, the all share index (actually following 500 shares), indices for specific industries, and so on.

Equivalent indices for other stock exchanges include the Dow Jones, NYSE composite, Nasdaq and Standard and Poors in the USA, Nikkei in Japan, Dax in Germany, CAC in France and Hang Seng in Hong Kong.

Table 4.2 (on page 34) shows an extract from a French stock exchange report. This gives the value of two common indices over the past three days, together with the highest and lowest values reached during the past year, and one estimate of the average yield and price to earnings (P/E) ratio.

Remember when looking at these indices that there is a difference between 'percentage' and 'percentage point'. Suppose that an index with a base value of 100 rises from 200 to 210 on a particular day. You can describe this as a rise of 'ten percentage points' (the number of points it rose) or 'five percent' (the rise as a percentage of the previous value).

5

SPREADING RISK

Risk and insurance

Financial markets are, by their nature, risky places. People forecast – or guess – what will happen in the future and invest their money accordingly. Their guesses may be right and they make a quick fortune; or they may be wrong and they lose.

Some speculators deliberately look for high-risk deals, to get the high potential rewards. Other organizations do not like working with so much risk, and look for ways of avoiding it. Pension funds, for example, have to guarantee long-term returns to their customers and thus prefer safer options.

One way of reducing the effect of risk is to take out insurance. This passes certain risks to someone else – normally an insurance company with enough resources to withstand any adverse consequences. If your house burns down, you would probably have difficulty finding the cash to rebuild it, but a large insurance company could suffer the loss without too much trouble.

General insurance companies take on risks from fire, theft, damage, and so on. In return, they get an income from two sources: they employ **actuaries** to calculate the risk, and then quote premiums that are, on average, higher than the likely cost of covering claims; and they invest the money collected as premiums until such time as they have to pay any claims.

Most insurance is actually arranged by **insurance brokers**, who are intermediaries between customers and the insurance companies. In theory, brokers use their expertise to find the best deals for their customers. In practice, the commissions they receive might affect the impartiality of their advice.

When a risk is too great for a single company, the original insurer can **reinsure** it, laying off some of the risk with other companies. This is the same principle used by bookmakers when they lay off very big bets. Reinsurance needs an active market place where the various companies can talk to each other. **Lloyd's of London** is the world's leading market place.

Lloyd's originally specialized in marine insurance, but developed into the main market for reinsurance. Its **members**, who are now a combination of rich individuals and other companies, are organized into **syndicates**. When a big policy appears, several syndicates join together to cover the whole deal.

Life assurance

General insurance companies cover damage to cars, houses, ships, and so on. Life assurance companies started by giving life insurance – paying up when the insured person died. Most of their business is now with term policies, which combine life insurance and savings. The assurance company collects premiums, which it invests in its **life funds**, and after some specified term it returns a lump sum – or continuing pension – to the customer.

The common feature of general insurance, life assurance and pension companies is that they collect money from customers a long time before they return it. This gives them huge amounts of cash to invest, making them the biggest investors on the stock exchange. But they have to be very careful with the way they invest their funds. Even when they think that a particular share will rise in value, they cannot risk putting too much into a single investment in case they are wrong. They spread their risk with a **balanced portfolio** – spreading money around rather than putting all their eggs in one basket. Usually they accept some balance of risk and security, with most investments being safe and giving lower, assured returns, while others are riskier but potentially more profitable.

Fund managers choose the range of shares and invest-ments that they think will give the best long-term returns. These fund managers are not equally successful in their choices, and there are significant differences in perfor-mance between companies and funds. This raises the inter-esting question of how you find the funds with the best managers. Unfortunately, there is no answer to this. Good performance in the past certainly does not guarantee good performance in the future. Perhaps you should consult a financial advisor or financial consultant – but remember that many of these are salespeople who are actually paid by the companies they recommend. One problem is that fund managers generally seem to perform worse than the general stock market. In other words, it would be better to invest in a random spread of shares than take the advice of a highly paid fund manager.

Unit trusts

Unlike the big companies, most of us cannot afford our own fund manager – but we still want to spread our risks and get a good long-term return. We can do this through **unit trusts**. These are managed funds that give a simple way of spreading a small amount of cash over a wide range of investments.

Finance companies sell thousands of different unit trusts, but they all work in roughly the same way. A fund manager chooses a range of investments, often with some focus, such as UK equities, property, small companies, utilities, and so on. Investors buy units of this fund. The fund manager pools the cash from a lot of investors, so that the fund is large enough to spread over a range of opportunities. Over time the fund should increase in value through dividends and capital growth, and the value of each unit increases.

As with shares, unit trusts have two quoted prices – a higher offer price at which you buy, and a lower bid price at which you sell. The difference between the two covers the administration costs and profits for the operators. You can find their price and yield in published tables, such as the extract given in Table 5.1.

The name of the fund often gives you an idea of its focus and aims, so something like 'UK growth' will probably focus

Table 5.1 Typical report of unit trust performance

Name	Initial Charge	Selling Price	Buying Price	Change On Day	Yield
UK growth	6.0	207.0	217.8	+1.0	0.88
Equity income	6.0	146.0	153.6	+0.1	0.83
Balanced growth	4.0	107.2	112.6	−0.2	1.31

on UK shares, with an emphasis on capital growth rather than high dividends. Most unit trusts have an initial charge, so as well as paying more to buy the unit trusts than to sell, you might also pay a 6 per cent charge when you buy the units. Sometimes there are periodic charges or exit charges when you sell, and these mean that you should only consider unit trusts as longer-term investments.

As you would expect, unit trusts do not perform equally well. There are two general strategies for managing them: **active funds** and **tracker funds**. With active funds, fund managers choose a range of investments that they think will perform well. They try to get better performance than the market as a whole – but unfortunately they often fail. Tracker funds choose a range of funds to track the average performance. Choosing shares in the FTSE 100, for example, will give a performance that tracks this index.

In general, unit trusts tend to emphasize safety rather than spectacular performance.

Other pooled investments

If you have a bit more cash to play with, you can spread your risks by joining an investment club. This is simply a group of people who pool an agreed amount of money and manage their own investments. These clubs can be quite successful, and an unpaid amateur fund manager can often outperform a highly paid professional. One note is that the club has to remain small, for otherwise it is legally required to become a limited company – **an investment trust**. These are companies whose sole purpose is to invest in other companies.

Successive governments have encouraged individual savings through a series of tax incentives. Currently, you can get some tax-free income through **Individual Savings**

Accounts (ISAs), of which there is a huge variety, often involving managed funds.

Derivatives

Another way of managing risks is through **derivatives**. This is a highly specialized area that deals in the future value of shares, bonds, currencies and commodities. It does not create any new products, but its business is derived from existing products. You can see how the derivatives market works by looking at an everyday commodity, such as cocoa.

Imagine that you run a chocolate factory. The easiest way of buying cocoa beans is to pay the current prices and get immediate delivery – rather like going into a shop. This is trading on the **spot market**. If you want a continuous supply of cocoa into the future, you could keep buying it on the spot market.

Unfortunately, the spot price is likely to vary with market conditions, and you might feel more secure if you knew how much the cocoa will cost for some time in the future. This would also benefit suppliers who would know exactly how much they will get. This is the purpose of the **futures** or **forward market**. It allows a company to buy a commodity at an agreed price for delivery some time in the future.

Typically, the futures market quotes a spot price, three month delivery, six month delivery, nine month delivery, and so on. If you need cocoa in six months' time, you can make a contract for six-month cocoa, pay a deposit, wait for delivery in six months' time, and then settle the payment. You have the security of knowing exactly how much the cocoa will cost, and the supplier has the security of a firm sale. But both of you are gambling – you that the spot price in six months' time will not be much lower, and the supplier that the spot price will not be much higher.

This element of risk means that two types of people are interested in forward buying: companies who want to hedge against price changes in their raw materials, and speculators who can make money from betting on future price changes.

You can easily see how speculators can make money from the futures market. In January, they might think that six-month cocoa is undervalued, and buy some for delivery in July. Then they could wait until July and, if the spot price is higher than the amount they paid, they make a profit by immediately selling their delivery of cocoa on the spot market. Alternatively, they might find that in April, three-month cocoa is expensive. Now they can sell their contract for delivery in July at the three-month price and make a profit. They never actually own the cocoa, but trade in contracts for future delivery. This is the basis of the derivatives market: it does not buy and sell cocoa, but it buys and sells contracts for future delivery of cocoa.

Table 5.2 shows an extract of forward cocoa prices. This shows the prices (in pounds per tonne) of cocoa delivered

Table 5.2 Illustration of forward commodity prices

1	2	3	4	5	6
	Price	Change On Day	High	Low	Volume
January	941	+1	945	939	520
March	949	–	953	943	1339
May	967	−1	972	962	847
August	985	−3	990	980	670
November	1003	−3	1010	1008	295
January	1015	−3	1020	1010	280

at different times in the future, how the prices have changed, and an indication of the volume of business.

Financial instruments

The derivatives market buys and sells **financial instruments**. Contracts for cocoa futures are one of these instruments, but the same principles apply to many other things. These are traded on different markets in London:

- metals – copper, lead, zinc, tin, silver and other 'hard commodities' – are traded on the **London Metal Exchange**;

- foodstuffs – cocoa, coffee, sugar, tea, jute and other 'soft commodities' – are traded on the **London Commodities Market**;

- oil products are traded in the **International Petroleum Exchange**;

- shipping, freight and some commodities are organized through the **Baltic Exchange**; and

- forward contracts and options are traded in the huge **London International Financial Futures and Options Exchange (LIFFE)**.

The forward market used to be dominated by commodities, but this has been overtaken by the **financial futures** market, which sets the future price for bonds, shares, currencies and other financial instruments. **Certificates of deposit**, for example, show how financial futures work. Suppose that a company has £500,000 in spare cash. It can deposit this with a bank, and if it guarantees to leave the money in for a year it gets a higher rate of interest. The company gets a certificate of deposit, saying how much money it will get back in a year's time. If they need cash before this, they can trade their certificate in the financial futures market.

One attraction of the derivatives market is that when buying a contract, investors do not put up the value of the contract, but only a deposit. They might, for example, put down a deposit of £50,000 on a contract to buy £1 million of bonds in three months' time. They assume that before they actually have to pay the £1 million, the price of the bonds will rise and they will sell the contract on to someone else. If the bond price rises to, say, £1.1 million, their £50,000 deposit makes a very healthy return. Here, a small amount of cash effectively controls a large contract value.

The drawback, of course, is that prices can fall as well as rise, and speculators then have to pay out more for a delivery than it is worth. If the spot value of bonds falls, at the end of three months our speculators might have to honour their contract and pay £1 million for bonds that are now only worth £500,000. Needless to say, such speculation in the derivatives market is a very risky business done by specialists with deep pockets.

Options

Options are similar to futures, in that people buy and sell things they do not actually own. **Share options** give you the right to buy or sell shares at a specified price over some period in the future.

If you think that a share is going to rise in value, you could, of course, buy some. This has the drawback that you could lose all the money you invest. An alternative is to buy an option on the shares. Suppose that a share has a value of 100p, but you think that it will rise over the next three months. Rather than buy the shares at 100p, you could buy an option on them. This might cost 10p a share – the

premium – and allow you to buy the shares for 110p at any time within the next three months. If the share price rises above 120p you can exercise your call option, buy the shares at 110p, and immediately sell them for a profit. If the share price does not rise enough, you do not exercise your option to buy, and only lose your premium.

In the same way, you might own some shares whose price you think will fall. Then you can pay a premium for a **put option**. This is a contract that gives you the option of selling the shares within, say, the next three months, at a fixed price. The premium here is a form of insurance in case the share price plummets.

6

GOVERNMENT BONDS

Government spending

The government collects money – largely from tax revenues – and spends it. Sometimes its income is less than its expenditure, and it borrows money from investors, thereby increasing the national debt. The trend over recent years is for the total amount owed by the government to rise in value, but fall as a percentage of gross national product.

Most of the government's borrowing is organized by the Bank of England through UK **government bonds** or **gilt-edged stock**, usually called **gilts**. These are effectively IOUs issued by the government for fixed amounts – usually £100, which is their **nominal**, **par** or **face value**. Most gilts have a fixed interest rate, or **coupon**, and a date when they will be **redeemed** or bought back at face value by the government. 'Treasury 9 per cent 2012' refers to a bond that pays 9 per cent until 2012 when it will be redeemed for £100. The redemption date can be up to 40 years in the future, and some bonds are undated, with no redemption date. Depending on the time to redemption, bonds are classified as:

- short-dated (or shorts), with less than five years to redemption;
- medium-dated, with five to 15 years to redemption; or
- long-dated (or longs), with more than 15 years to redemption.

Every year the government issues new bonds to cover both its current borrowing needs and to replace older bonds that have matured.

When the government issues gilts to the primary market, it might issue them at slightly above or below their face value – at a premium or at a discount – depending on market conditions. After they are issued, you can buy and sell bonds in the secondary gilts market. The price of a bond depends on several factors, such as inflation rates, growth of earnings, number of gilts issued, economic forecasts and so on, but by far the dominant factor is the prevailing interest rate.

If you buy a £100 bond with a coupon of 10 per cent, you get £10 of interest a year. If the prevailing interest rate falls to 5 per cent, you would now have to invest £200 to get an income of £10 a year. In other words, people would be willing to pay £200 for your bond and still get a return of 5 per cent. The value of your bond has risen from £100 to £200 and you can sell it to make a capital gain. Clearly, the price of gilts is going to fall when interest rates rise, and their price rises when interest rates fall. Then the overall return is a combination of interest and capital gains (or, of course, losses).

Table 6.1 shows an extract from a typical report on UK gilts prices.

Table 6.1   Illustration of gilt prices

1	2	3	4	5	6	7	8
Name	Notes	Interest Yield	Redemp-tion Yield	Price	+/−	Annual High	Annual Low
Treas 8% 2009		6.63	5.28	120.68	−0.18	132.91	114.73

From the table, you can see that:

- Column 1 gives the name of the bond. Most bonds are called 'treasury' or 'exchequer' followed by their coupon and redemption date. The name has very little significance, and 'Treas 8% 2009' simply refers to a gilt bond with a coupon of 8% which will be redeemed in 2009. Some of the bonds have two redemption dates, and the government can choose to redeem at any point between them.

- Column 2 gives any relevant notes, perhaps saying if the price is real or is just an indicator.

- Column 3 is the interest yield. Remember that the coupon is based on the par value, so this gilt gives 8% interest on a par value of £100. At present, each £100 bond costs £120.68 (shown in Column 5), so the actual interest yield is:

$$\frac{\text{interest rate}}{\text{market price}} \times 100 = \frac{8 \times 100}{120.68} = 6.63\%$$

- Column 4 is the redemption yield. The government will redeem the bond in 2009 for £100, regardless of its market price at that point. As you would expect, the closer the date is to redemption, the closer the market value approaches the redemption value. This bond has nine years to run, and during that time its value will decline from £120.68 to £100. In other words, there is a capital loss of £20.68. This annual loss has to be subtracted from the interest yield to give a more realistic figure for the return. This is calculated using compound rates, with the adjusted yield quoted as 5.28 per cent. If the market price is below the par value, there is a capital gain, and the interest yield is adjusted upwards.

- Column 5 gives the current bond price in pounds. This is the middle price for a nominal £100 bond at the close of the last day's trading – the purchase price is slightly above this, and the selling price is slightly lower.

- Column 6 shows how the market price changed during the last day of trading.

- Columns 7 and 8 give an idea of the price changes by showing the 52-week high and low price.

Newspapers report a wide range of UK gilts and government bonds from other countries. Always remember that when you make international comparisons you have to consider a lot more than the basic prices. In an extreme case, you might be offered bonds from, say, tsarist Russia, imperial China, or colonial South America. You should realize that these have no commercial value, do not pay interest and will never be redeemed by the issuing country. Their only value is that some look good when framed and hanging on a wall.

Other types of bond

The market for gilts is fairly quiet. The government issues and redeems them, and in between they earn interest and are traded in the stock exchange. But there are many other types of bond issued by different organizations, and these range from the very safe to the very risky. The most common types are shorter-term **local authority bonds** (or corporation loans), and **corporate bonds** (loan stocks or debentures). You also find income bonds from life assurance companies, property and commodity bonds, and bonds issued by foreign governments. The UK government itself issues several kinds of bonds including National Savings, which have variable interest, and Premium bonds, which give monthly prizes.

The details of these bonds vary slightly, but in principle they all work in a similar way, being fixed term IOUs. Sometimes the interest rate is variable, with the yield linked to the retail price index. In return for this safeguard against inflation, the coupon is usually lower.

Corporate bonds

Corporate bonds are the same in principle as gilts, but they are inevitably more risky. The government, in one form or another, will almost certainly be with us in 25 years time – but can we be so sure about even the safest company? For this reason, the coupon offered with corporate bonds is usually higher – typically half a per cent higher.

One important benefit of bonds appears when the issuing company runs into difficulties. Bond-holders (and just about everyone else) get paid before shareholders, and they are more likely to get something before the cash runs out. This means that bonds are less risky than shares and they receive correspondingly lower returns. On the other hand, when a company is going through good times, it is better to hold shares than bonds, as they get more of the profits.

Security is obviously important for bonds. If the issuing company is less secure, it has to offer a higher coupon, and

Table 6.2 Illustration of ratings and yield

1	2	3	4	5	6	7	8	9
	Redemption						Day's	Month's
Name	Date	Coupon	S&P Rating	Moody's Rating	Bid Price	Yield	Change Yield	Change Yield
Sweden	02/01	5.000	AA+	Aa1	101.103	3.92	−0.04	+0.07
Powergen	07/09	5.00	A	A2	90.951	6.29	−0.13	+0.40
BAT Intfin	07/06	5.375	A	A2	96.253	6.08	−0.13	+0.22
Remy Cointrea	07/05	10.000	B+	B1	107.475	8.29	−0.13	+0.35

some companies have to offer very high yields for their 'junk bonds'. If you are careful and lucky, these can give high returns, but you have to be aware of the risks. To help assess these, you can look up a company's credit rating. There are several independent credit ratings for companies, with the best known being Standard and Poor's (S&P) and Moody's. These rate organizations from **AAA** – a triple A rating – for the safest organizations, downwards for more risky investments. The ratings are quite severe, and you should not imagine that companies with less than a triple A rating are risky. In reality, few governments achieve this highest rating. Table 6.2 shows an extract from a typical report and you can see from columns 4 and 5 that even the Swedish government does not get the highest rating.

One interesting point is that companies need not issue bonds in the country in which they are based. A French company, for example, might issue bonds in London. For some reason, bonds issued by foreign companies in sterling in the UK are called 'bulldog bonds' (with equivalent 'yankees' in New York, and 'samurais' in Tokyo).

7

DEALING INTERNATIONALLY

Arbitrage

Finance markets are completely international, and money follows an opportunity anywhere in the world. The official hours of the London Stock Exchange are 8.30 am to 4.30 pm, which means that it opens just as the Tokyo stock exchange is closing, and it closes just as the New York stock exchange opens. As you can imagine, **after-hours trading** continues, and international deals are made at any convenient time.

Sometimes two markets get a little out of phase and a particular investment might have a different price in two different markets. Perhaps a share has a higher price in New York than London, in which case investors will move quickly to buy in London and sell in New York. This kind of deal is known as **arbitrage**, and it brings prices back into line. Although they operate separately, there are clear links between the different markets.

Euromarkets

The huge international market in bonds issued by governments and other organizations is traded in the **Euromarket**. The term 'Euromarket' is historical and is now rather misleading: there is no formal market, and deals need not be in Europe or even in a European currency.

The term started when US companies began depositing dollars in European banks, and these became 'Eurodollars'. Later German marks deposited in British banks became Euromarks, and the Japanese introduced Euroyen. Now Eurocurrencies refer to any deposits in currencies outside their country of origin, and these are traded in Euromarkets. The name now describes the type of transaction, which might be, say, a transaction in US dollars on the Hong Kong market.

The attraction of Euromarkets is that they avoid some of the rules and regulations that control local financial markets. When, for example, the US imposed controls on interest rates, companies could get around these by trading in dollars on the international markets.

Euromarkets now offer a similar range of services to national markets. Companies borrow money by issuing bonds in a Eurocurrency – **Eurobonds** – and these transactions passed US $1 trillion by 1997. In the same way, an increasing number of companies are raising equity by issuing shares in the international market rather than in their domestic stock exchange. (Be careful here. Bonds are increasingly issued in euros – the currency; these are euro bonds but are not necessarily Eurobonds.)

Exchange rates

Most of us do not deal in the Euromarket, and our main contact with international finance is through the currency exchange rates. Here we enter an entirely new world of unpredictable behaviour and dramatic changes with no apparent cause.

Major international currencies have floating exchange rates, which means that they rely on market forces to set their values. Actually, they rely on market forces with help from governments, central banks and other concerned bodies.

If a country exports more than it imports, it has a positive **balance of payments**. Exports must eventually be paid for in local currencies, and if Germany exports more than it imports, outside customers must eventually pay in marks. This creates a demand for marks and the value rises against other currencies.

Some people suggest that this leads to a self-regulating system. A balance of trade surplus leads to a strong economy and a high valued currency. This makes the country's exports more expensive, and its imports cheaper. The balance of trade suffers, the currency weakens, and – in the long-term – stability returns. Looking around the world, you might find this argument rather unconvincing.

One of the problems is that there are two parallel trades, one of goods – the **visible trade** – and one of finance and other services – the **invisible trade**. The strength of a currency depends on both the visible trade (which must be paid for in the currency) and the demand for the currency from investors.

Even if the visible trade is not particularly healthy, a government can increase the value of its currency by, say, raising interest rates to encourage investors.

Government intervention

Governments have their own objectives for their currency, which are not necessarily the same as those of international dealers. If a currency falls too low, imports get more expensive and a population's prosperity can be affected. A government might try to stop its currency falling by instructing its central bank to offer support. This means using its reserves to buy currency, thus increasing demand and raising the price. This option only works in the short term, as the central bank will soon run out of funds, and even a consortium of central banks cannot overcome a long-term trend.

As an alternative to buying currency, the government can raise the official interest rate. This gives investors a higher return, and they will transfer funds into the country from areas with lower rates. Unfortunately, domestic industries now have to pay higher interest charges, and this will cause even more problems in the longer term.

Interest rates are also linked to inflation, so investors have to look at the total yield they can expect, bearing in mind the combination of interest earned and changing value of the currency. A low interest rate with a rising currency value (such as in Japan) can still give a high yield; on the other hand, a high interest rate with a falling currency value (such as in Brazil) can give a low yield.

Comparing currencies

Every currency is continually moving in relation to others. Often there is not any clear pattern, so the pound might strengthen against the dollar but weaken against the yen. You can see comparisons of currency values in tables of 'exchange cross rates'. Table 7.1 shows a fragment of one such table, showing the number of Belgian francs, Danish

Table 7.1 Part of a table of exchange rates

	BFr	DKr	FFr	DM	I£	L	FI	NKr	Es	Pta
UK £	64.22	11.84	10.44	3.113	1.254	3082	3.508	13.07	319.1	264.9
US $	39.21	7.231	6.375	1.901	0.765	1882	2.142	7.977	194.9	161.7

Table 7.2 Pound forward rates

1	2	3	4	5	6	7	8	9	10
	Closing Mid-point	Change on Day	Bid/ Offer Spread	Day's Mid High	Day's Mid Low	One Month	Three Months	One Year	Bank of England Index
Sweden	13.7986	+0.0379	878–093	13.8474	13.7640	13.7721	13.7165	13.5045	82.3
Switzerland	2.5590	+0.0026	574–606	2.5732	2.5564	2.5499	2.5320	2.4529	103.9

kroner, and so on it takes to buy a pound and a US dollar. The only point with these tables is that they have slightly different formats, and you have to read the descriptions carefully. For example, they usually show both the number of Belgian francs needed to buy a pound, and the number of pounds needed to buy a Belgian franc – make sure that you get them the right way around!

Changing rates

The cross rates give an instant picture of each currency – usually the middle prices on the spot market. They do not show the movements over time. If you plot the spot value of, say, the pound against the dollar over time, you can see the long-term trends. An alternative is to look at the forward markets, which give the expected future values of currencies. Table 7.2 shows part of a table for the forward value of the pound against two random currencies.

From Table 7.2, you can see that:

- Columns 2 and 3 show the middle price of a pound in Swedish kronor and Swiss francs, and the amount this has changed since the end of the last working day.

- Column 4 shows the spread between bid and offer price. Only the last three decimal places are given and, remembering that the bid price is lower than the offer price, you can see that the spread for Swedish kronor is 13.7878 to 13.8093. Not surprisingly, the average of these two is 13.7986, as reported in column 2.

- Columns 5 and 6 show the highest and lowest middle prices for the day.

- Columns 7, 8 and 9 show the middle price of futures – so a pound delivered in three months time will cost 13.7165 kronor.

You can get a more general feel for the changing value of currency by calculating an index of its relative value. Column 10 shows how the pound has moved against a bundle of currencies. The most important variations are those with our major trading partners, so the Bank of England calculates the **trade-weighted index**. This finds the variations of the pound against other currencies, and weights them according to the amount of trade between the countries. The index was set at 100 in 1990, and currently has a value around 105, showing that the pound has risen by five per cent in relative terms.

The 30 Minutes Series

Titles available are: *30 Minutes* . . .

Available from all good booksellers.
For further information on the series, please contact:

Kogan Page, 120 Pentonville Road, London N1 9JN
Tel: 020 7278 0433 Fax: 020 7837 6348

www.kogan-page.co.uk